T0194336

STARTING *to* FINISH

STARTING
to FINISH

A Doctoral Journey

Yolanda Stokes, EdD

WESTBOW
PRESS®
A DIVISION OF THOMAS NELSON
& ZONDERVAN

WestBow Press books may be ordered through
booksellers or by contacting:

WestBow Press
A Division of Thomas Nelson & Zondervan
1663 Liberty Drive
Bloomington, IN 47403
www.westbowpress.com
1 (866) 928-1240

ISBN: 978-1-9736-6359-1 (sc)
ISBN: 978-1-9736-6360-7 (e)

Library of Congress Control Number: 2019906980

Print information available on the last page.

WestBow Press rev. date: 6/17/2019

This guide has been prepared for anyone who desires to complete a doctoral journey.

Not unlike building a house, you must do so on solid ground so as the waves beat vehemently against your house; you can withstand the trials and challenges which await you.

Matthew 7:24–27 (NKJV)

CONTENTS

FOREWORD
By Paige Stokes

In the spring of 2015, my mom decided that it was time to go back to school to start her doctorate. While she'd completed her bachelor's and master's degrees more than twenty years prior, she chose to jump back into the world of academia. Though it took some time to adjust to the demands school required, she excelled as both a full-time student and employee.

She started writing this book shortly after receiving the dean's signature for her dissertation. It's truly admirable that the first thing that she wanted to do once completing her degree was help others who were in the process. She would often encourage herself during challenging times by saying, "It's not supposed to be easy. If it were easy, everyone would be doing it."

While you may face setbacks from time to time, turn to the Bible for encouragement. Second Chronicles 15:7 says, "But as for you, be strong and do not give up, for your work will be rewarded" (NIV).

Our prayer is that this guide provides additional light as you work toward completing your program. Proverbs 3:5–6 says, "Trust in the Lord with all your heart and lean not on your own understanding; in all your ways submit to him, and he will make your paths straight" (NIV).

You are almost done. You're one step closer to being called "doctor." As my mom said while working on her degree, "I'm starting to finish."

PREFACE

Have you ever found yourself in a position, full of passion, ready to overcome what appeared to be insurmountable challenges, only to realize you lacked the skills and resources necessary to defeat your Goliath? At several points in my life, that was me. God put on my heart a yearning to help others. At those times, I was not sure exactly how I would do that, but I was willing to listen.

My favorite scripture for many years has been Hebrews 11:1: "Now faith is the substance of things hoped for, the evidence of things not seen" (KJV). For me, this scripture does two things. First, it focuses on the now. Faith is now. Second, it speaks to future events—those things hoped for, those things not yet seen.

When paired with Luke 17:6—"If you have faith as small as a mustard seed, you can say to this mulberry tree, 'Be uprooted and planted in the sea,' and it will obey you" (NIV)—it is not too difficult to realize how the lack of skills and resources has little to do with fulfilling the calling placed on your life.

If you are reading this and asking yourself what any of this has to do with enabling the completion of a doctoral journey, I suggest you keep reading. I intend to offer practical tips to help you complete the faith journey you have begun—or are about to embark upon—through the use of divine downloads so you can successfully finish what you started.

CHAPTER 1

Reflection

David and Jonah

David, a mighty warrior in the Bible, was a man after God's heart and someone committed to performing God's will, as we learned in Acts 13:22. He found himself in situations where he realized he could not continue without help—the kind of support only God can provide. In one instance, when King Achish and the Philistine commanders were preparing for battle in Jezreel, David and his warriors were asked to return to Philistine territory.

The Philistine leaders knew David was out of favor with King Saul and feared he might try to regain his master's approval by ridding the earth of members of the Philistine army. When David and his men returned to Ziklag, they found the town destroyed and their families taken captive. Following a long period of weeping, David's army considered stoning him, but David found strength in the Lord, consulting God for direction, and pursued and overtook his enemies, ultimately recovering all the goods previously stolen (1 Samuel 29:1–30:20).

Now let's turn our attention to Jonah. Jonah, a prophet of the Lord, was directed to go to the city of Nineveh and preach against it, exposing the wickedness that had manifested broadly. Instead of seizing this opportunity to show himself faithful to the God that he served, Jonah decided to run away, heading to Tarshish aboard a ship. His disobedience prompted God to stir the winds, creating a violent storm. It was not too long before Jonah drew the "short straw," exposing to the others aboard that his disobedience had caused the storm. At his request, Jonah was tossed overboard, and the sea calmed. Soon after, a big fish swallowed Jonah, and for the next three days and nights, it journeyed him back to Nineveh so that he could fulfill what God originally called him to do (Jonah 1:1–17).

Ultimately, you have a choice. You can choose to take on each of the battles this doctoral journey has to offer and follow in David's footsteps to find strength in the Lord. Or you can run away, as Jonah did, from the purpose God has called you to perform. So which will it be?

What the Dissertation Process Is Really Like

I recently heard a comment from a doctoral student who was still focused on the day-to-day challenges of the coursework designed to prepare students for the dissertation itself. Her thought was, "I have managed large projects before, and as a result, the dissertation experience should not be much different." Let's be clear. Writing a dissertation is not equivalent to just any large project. One PhD graduate compared the dissertation process to hazing, the abusive practices used to initiate Greek fraternity and sorority members, or the "jumping-in" methods used by gang members. The process has also been described as one that requires use of "extensive resources from others who are involved in the process" (Grant and Osanloo 2014, 12).

Eager beavers choosing to embark on the doctoral experience may consider themselves self-starters, conquerors, or overcomers—all of which may be true. However, new learners should be aware that "the dissertation can make procrastinators out of non-procrastinators and drive chronic procrastinators to despair: it can feel completely overwhelming" (Morrison Straforini 2015, 298). In light of that, I propose that you need to "precrastinate" to stay ahead, remain committed, and finish what you started: the acquisition of a doctoral degree.

Let's reflect on the parable of the ten virgins

as an example for understanding the gravity of procrastination implications. The story shares the fate of ten virgins, five who were wise and five who were not. As the women awaited the arrival of their bridegroom, who was a long time coming, the lamps of the five foolish virgins began to run short on oil. In need of more, they were forced to find vendors who could sell them the needed oil. While they were away, however, the bridegroom arrived and welcomed the five wise virgins into his wedding banquet. When the five foolish virgins finally returned and desired to enter, they were turned away. The lack of planning for the amount of lamp oil needed for a longer-than-expected waiting period prevented the five foolish virgins from attending the banquet. Instead, the bridegroom dismissed them by commenting, "Truly, I tell you, I do not know you" (Matthew 25:1–13 ESV). The consequence of their procrastination was fatally extended beyond the banquet into eternity.

At the onset of the doctoral program, learners

engage in environments with other students. In many cases, those attending are at or near the same place in the program. Classes are larger, mimicking prior graduate program configurations. Over time, however, the number of learners per course reduces as learners achieve the necessary milestones along the defined paths for their particular programs of study. My first three courses had well over twenty students. We unified around a sense of comradery and connectedness. We offered our perspectives and encouraged each other as a reminder that we were not alone. Conversely, I was the only person in my last three courses. That could have been because some students had graduated sooner, and others may have chosen not to graduate at all. Regardless of the reason, there was no one left to inspire, encourage, or motivate me. The opening story of David following the battle of Ziklag was a reality for me on more than one occasion, when I had to encourage myself in the Lord to continue moving forward. I persevered. I pocketed my oil.

What You Should Consider before Saying "I Do"

When I began the doctoral program, a PhD friend let me know that when I graduated, my master's degree would seem insignificant. On hearing that, I was offended. I simply could not wrap my brain around how that statement would have any truth for me, mainly because of how hard I had worked to obtain that degree. I had given birth to my first child and was five months pregnant with my second at the time of commencement, and had been working full time throughout the program. That part of my life will always have meaning!

While I do not agree that your other graduate work will seem insignificant, assuredly, you will be a different person following the conclusion of your chosen program of study, even more than you could ever imagine. You will have gained an abundance of new information based on your research, you will have added to existing bodies of knowledge, and you will have the distinction of the title of *doctor*. You will also be faced with several obstacles, such as tension resulting from missed celebrations, professional pressures, and strained relationships. Further, you will have to balance commitments, academic skills, health, and other financial difficulties (Drury and Charles 2016). Students often struggle with the emotional energy, time, and dedication required to complete dissertation requirements (Burkard, Knox, DeWalt, Fuller, Hill, and Schlosser 2014). At the end of it all, you will have proven to yourself that you are a survivor.

Given the challenges that lie ahead, it is no wonder that only nearly 2 percent of Americans have a doctoral degree (Wilson 2017). The impending journey is daunting and not suitable for the faint of heart, the Jonahs of the world. Writing occurs one word, one sentence, and one page at a time. Be patient with yourself, as the writing and rewriting process can be disturbing and tiresome. I encourage you not to become weary and miss out on the harvest that awaits you (Galatians 6:9). Before you agree to begin a graduate program at this level, understand that a supportive sense of community positively influences the students' doctoral experiences (Byrd 2016). Therefore, build a network around you of people who understand that your journey is only for a season.

Remember,

There is a time for everything, and a season for every activity under the heavens: a time to be born and a time to die, a time to plant and a time to uproot, a time to kill and a time to heal, a time to tear down and a time to build, a time to weep and a time to laugh, a time to mourn and a time to dance, a time to scatter stones and a time to gather them, a time to embrace and a time to refrain from embracing, a time to search and a time to give up, a time to keep and a time to throw away, a time to tear and a time to mend, a time to be silent and a time to speak, a time to love and a time to hate, a time for war and a time for peace. (Ecclesiastes 3:1–22 NIV)

Once you have established that you are ready, willing, and able to operate in mustard-seed faith (Matthew 17:20), then say "I do" to the invitation to begin a doctoral program. Say, "I will finish what I started." Say, "I am ready to don the whole armor of God and join the fight like David and his men."

CHAPTER 2

The Next Step

The Fall of Jericho

We pick up this story in Joshua 6, where Joshua was met with a commander of the Lord's army. At that time, Joshua was told that he and the Israelites had victory over the king and people of Jericho, who had a false sense of security because they lived in a city secured by high walls that appeared impenetrable. The instructions given to Joshua involved preparation. He was told to march around the city one time for six days with the priests and all his armed men. On the seventh day, however, they were to march around the city seven times, with the priests blowing their trumpets. At the sound of the long trumpet blast and a loud war cry from the entire army, the walls of Jericho would fall.

Although the instructions that were provided did not seem entirely logical, the army and priests were obedient to the commands given to Joshua. Each day for six days they marched around Jericho one time. On the seventh day, they marched around Jericho's walls seven times. Following the long blast of the trumpet and a loud shout, Jericho's walls collapsed, and the Israel army took the city by force.

You might be asking yourself, "What does the fall of Jericho have to do with me?" To address that question, here are a few key points for you to understand:

- Instructions from your chair or other committee members that you receive may not always seem relevant. Follow them anyway.

You do not yet have the wisdom to realize that your tree is part of a much larger forest. If you are passionate about doing things your way, find other scholars who agree with you. Remember that there is strength in numbers. Your opinion alone does not carry the same weight as the combined opinion of other doctors who have already gone where you are going.

- Maintain a keen sense of stick-with-it-ness. Completion of the doctoral experience far more closely resembles a marathon than a short sprint.
- Shout! Allow yourself to release emotions to relieve stress, celebrate successes, and move ahead.

The Research Topic

An early step in the process is to determine what you are planning to study. What problem are you attempting to solve? Why is it important? Where is your value add? Frankly, who cares? Maybe you have put some thought into this subject already, which is great. If, you have not, however, doing so is your next step. Consider that you should have some passion for the research because the two of you will have years to get acquainted. If you are overly enamored with your research topic, however, you run the risk of introducing unwanted bias, especially during the analysis and results phases. Conversely, if you are lukewarm on the chosen topic, you may tire prematurely and discontinue the journey altogether. Choose wisely.

Gregor and Hevner (2013) cautioned researchers to ensure they had a clear understanding of their proposed research contributions and appropriate use of the chosen design theory. Ensuring alignment and "fit" throughout the dissertation process increases the reliability and validity of the research. Since several new terms have been introduced, let me take a moment to shed light in a few areas.

- **Alignment:** Threading a common theme throughout each of the research components (e.g., variables, research questions, conceptual/ theoretical framework(s), etc.). The bottom line with alignment is that you are striving to ensure that all things related to your research are connected. Imagine a straight line. Ask yourself, "Is there a common component that each of the research components has in connection with that line?"

- **Reliability:** Reliability and repeatability are friends. Consider sharing a sugar cookie recipe with a buddy. If you both followed an identical recipe, your cookies should taste so similar that your taste buds would be unable to discern whether you or your friend made them. When you are unable to tell the difference, you know that your recipe is reliable.

- **Validity:** Validity relates particularly to your chosen research method, design, and instrumentation. Assume that the fastest speed for a sports car on an open highway is two hundred miles per hour. If you tried to compare the sports car speed with that of a minivan, you would have an invalid comparison, since the pace of these vehicles cannot be appropriately examined. With validity, the assertions that you make should adequately relate to the components in your study.

You will work to synthesize details from empirical journal articles and uncover gaps as you home in on your "doable" topic. An example follows for those who might have questions on what is meant by doable. For instance, while you may have interest in alien life on Mars, since you are unable to interview aliens to obtain firsthand testimonials, it would be advisable for you to shift gears quickly before valuable time is lost.

Planning and Preparation

Ready yourself for tremendous amounts of reading. We will cover how to make the best use of your time in the next chapter. For now, understand that Zientek and Thompson (2009) noted that "conducting a study is analogous to detective work" (350). Much like a detective, roll out your crime scene barricade tape to partition your study area, obtain your tools (e.g., journal articles, makers, Post-it notes, etc.) and get to work.

Morrison Straforini (2015) observed that a dissertation should be interesting, original, and doable. The analogy provided was that the dissertation itself should resemble the fable of Goldilocks and the three bears, in that the research product "should not be too big or too little, and must be something the student can claim as his or her own territory without risking accusations of trespassing" (Morrison Straforini 2015, 309). The challenge becomes how to pursue a publishable work in academia that is "quality stamped" (Tribe and Tunariu 2016, 50) without losing sight of defined dissertation requirements that include succinct synthesization of research from others.

Finding Your Voice

Writing for academia is unlike writing for any other institution or profession. I would encourage you to incorporate style guide (American Psychological Association (APA), Modern Language Association (MLA)) requirements throughout your coursework based on your school's prerequisites so that when you are hard at work on your dissertation, you have received years of practice and feedback from your professors. Basthomi (2015) discussed discourse competence, which is associated with the ability to generate written and spoken logical language that is connected and coherent. Finding your voice is finding your writing competence.

Dissertation Components

Dissertations from university to university are not structured identically. There are, however, similarities. Initial pages in the manuscript include the title page, table of contents, abstract (if desired), acknowledgments (if desired), and lists of figures and tables. The body incorporates chapters that offer an introduction, literature review, methods justification, results, analysis, discussion, and conclusions. A reference or bibliography section, in addition to appendices, generally completes the required components.

You should ensure you understand the requirements for your journey in each of these areas long before you begin your work. Ensure that you intimately understand how best to identify an appropriate theoretical/conceptual framework, research questionnaires, research assumptions, limitations, and delimitations.

Dissertation Defense

The sound of the words *dissertation defense* places you mentally in a place of preservation—a posture where you ready yourself for battle. If you consider the defense nothing more than a scholarly conversation, you might find that not only are the words easier on the ear, but they help you better understand that you will have an opportunity to discuss your research with other like-minded professionals (i.e., your committee) who have served as your advocates throughout the program.

Chen (2014) explained that demonstrating knowledge in a defense in a necessary step in the process. Prost, Malleret, and Schöpfel (2015) stated that when research is done appropriately and correctly, future researchers and studies benefit from the use of prior efforts. Not unlike in the prior "Goldilocks and the Three Bears" example, do your part to find the "just right" connections throughout your research. Use those same connections to substantiate your research during the defense.

CHAPTER 3

The Secret Sauce

Moses and the Burning Bush

In Exodus 3, we learned that God called to Moses from a burning bush. The Lord mentioned that he had heard the cries of the Israelites as a result of the oppression imposed by Pharaoh and his leaders. In chapter 4, God began to instruct Moses on the signs and wonders he would perform in Pharaoh's presence to encourage him to let the Israelites depart from Egypt so they could hold a festival for Him in the wilderness. The Lord further said He would harden Pharaoh's heart so that he would not let His people go. Pharaoh would have to be compelled with God's mighty displays of signs and wonders.

We now know that Moses was given foresight. He had the opportunity to hear directly from God the events to come. He knew Aaron would be with him to help communicate the forthcoming events. This chapter is intended to provide you with foresight—or the secret sauce—that will give you practical tips that if applied will aid in the success of your doctoral experience.

Practical Tips to Aid in Your Success

- **Dictation**. Enabling dictation on your laptop will permit you to hear typed words on the page. While this tip may appear inconsequential, frequently when we read our writing, we mentally add words that never existed. Listening to the typed words will allow you to quickly correct areas of opportunity.

Dictation is also an excellent way to consume volumes of information from journal articles faster.

- **Grammar checker:** Unless you were an English major or a professional editor, you will likely find value in Grammarly. It is a free grammar checker to help you improve your writing. I encourage you to purchase the premium version, which reveals critical errors not available in the free version. The upgrade is not very expensive and is worth it!

- **Citation checker:** Become familiar with a citation checker to ensure that your citations meet your university's standards (e.g., APA, MLA). There are several available (e.g., Recite Works, EasyBib) for you to research to determine the most suitable product based on its available feature set.

- **Reference organizer:** Find a tool that can help you organize your references. A few examples are Mendeley Desktop, EndNote, and BibDesk.

While this may seem like an option, you will find that keeping track of literally hundreds of sources in a spreadsheet becomes unwieldy quickly.

- **Colored outline:** It is *imperative* for you to start this process with the first article that you read. The idea here is to create an outline of the literature review portion of your dissertation. Color code each section of the outline (e.g., I, II, III) a different color (e.g., red, blue, green, etc.). Create the necessary details (e.g., A, B) for each of the major sections as needed. As you read articles, highlight the sections according to the colors identified in the outline. Once you have done this, writing the literature review will be far more straightforward.

- **Understand your methodology:** Regardless of which method you believe is the best option for your study, ensure that other researchers agree with you. Once you have identified your chosen method, you need to spend ample amounts of time understanding its pros and cons, as well as the rationale for your choice. Each of these points require support from reputable journal articles. Become an expert!

- **Activate search engines:** Using keywords of your study, utilize search engines, such as EBSCOhost, Google Scholar, your school's library software, and others, to obtain potential empirical journal articles to contribute to your research project. Some students might find it helpful to create temporary email accounts to help manage the abundance of email traffic. Follow authors who have researched your area of interest. Finally, be mindful of each article's date. Universities have requirements for recent versus older source material. Following those rules at the onset will save you angst later.

- **Hire an editor:** If you believe you will need assistance with fine-tuning your academic writing before publishing your final dissertation, find an editor who has experience with scholarly writing at this level. Not all editors are created equally. Invest your time in finding a person who is suitable for your project before you invest your money.

- **Hire a tutor:** If you believe you will need assistance in thoroughly understanding statistics for quantitative studies, as an example, find someone who can explain them to you in a manner that you can easily comprehend. If you are not comfortable after a session or two, find someone else. Many companies offer free or reduced prices for on-demand mini-courses or training. If you can succinctly identify your questions, your tutoring experience may be free of charge.

- **Find a content expert:** Do your homework when searching for a content expert. Consider doctors who are not only in your field of study but may have created a survey instrument that you would like to use. I recall communicating with individuals across the globe for authorization to use their materials. You might be surprised how receptive people are to you when they are approached with right intentions.

- **APA settings:** Change the settings in the tools that you plan to use (e.g., Microsoft, SPSS, etc.) to benefit you most while you write versus once you have completed the process. If you are unsure of the most beneficial settings, seek YouTube for help and other experts to ease this part of your journey.

In Closing

As I mentioned at the onset of this writing, my heartfelt purpose was to create a guide that others could use to enable them to complete their doctoral experience. I faced a number of challenges throughout my program, including two major surgeries, four job changes, graduating two daughters from their undergraduate engineering degree programs, driving across country twice to move each of them into their permanent locations, and adjusting to my new role as "sofa girl" as I segregated myself for three and a half years to complete my work. Likely, you have had, or will have, similar struggles. Don't give up. Consider that it is far simpler to quit than to finish what you started. Finishing what you started, however, will provide you with years of immeasurable gratitude.

I cannot recall the number of times that I considered quitting, but I would always remind myself that I do not know how to quit. I am just not wired that way. My heavenly Father did not make me that way. Instead, He reminded me that:

- I am thoroughly equipped for all good works (2 Timothy 3:17)
- I am empowered with wisdom to resolve challenges because he gives me witty ideas, concepts, and inventions (Proverbs 8:12)

- I can do all things through Christ who strengthens me (Philippians 4:13)
- I am a new creature predestined for greatness (2 Corinthians 5:17)

What are you going to do with what He told you?

BIBLIOGRAPHY

Basthomi, Yazid. 2015. "Examining Research Spaces in Doctoral Prospectuses." *TEFLIN Journal, 20*(2), 140–158. Retrieved from http://journal.teflin.org/index.php/journal

Burkard, Alan. W., Sarah. Knox, Terri. DeWalt, Shauna. Fuller, Clara. Hill, and Lewis. Z. Schlosser. 2014. "Dissertation Experiences of Doctoral Graduates from Professional Psychology Programs." *Counselling Psychology Quarterly, 27*(1), 19–54. doi:10.1080/09515070.2013.821596

Byrd, Jeremy. C. 2016. "Understanding the Online Doctoral Learning Experience: Factors that Contribute to Students' Sense of Community." *Journal of Educators Online, 13*(2), 102–135. Available from https://www.thejeo.com/

Chen, Shuhua. 2014. Balancing Knowing and Not-Knowing: An Exploration of Doctoral Candidates' Performance of Researcher Selves in the Dissertation Defence. *Assessment and Evaluation in Higher Education, 39*(3), 364–379. doi:10.1080/02602938.2013.834876

Drury, Helen., and Cassily Charles. 2016. Overcoming Disadvantage, Achieving success: What Helps. *Journal of Academic Language and Learning, 10*(2), A48–A69. Available from http://journal.aall.org.au/index.php/jall/index

Grant, Cynthia, and Azadeh Osanloo. 2014. Understanding, Selecting, and Integrating a Theoretical Framework in Dissertation Research: Creating the Blueprint for Your "House". *Administrative Issues Journal: Education, Practice, And Research, 4*(2), 12–26. doi: 10.5929/2014.4.2.9

Gregor, Shirley, and Alan R. Hevner. 2013. Positioning and Presenting Design Science Research for Maximum Impact. *Management Information Systems: MIS Quarterly, 37*(2), 337–355. Retrieved from http://misq.org/

Morrison Straforini, Carol. 2015. Dissertation as Life Chapter: Managing Emotions, Relationships, and Time. *Journal of College Student Psychotherapy, 29*(4), 296–313. doi:10.1080 /87568225.2015.1074021

Prost, Hélène., Cécile Malleret,, and Joachim Schöpfel. 2015. Hidden Treasures: Opening Data in PhD Dissertations in Social Sciences and Humanities. *Journal of Librarianship and Scholarly Communication, 3*(2), 1–19. doi:10.7710/2162-3309.1230

Tribe, Rachel., and Aneta Tunariu. 2016. Turning Your Dissertation into a Publishable Journal Article. *Counselling Psychology Review, 31*(1), 50–58. Retrieved from http://roar.uel.ac.uk

Wilson, Reid. 2017. Census: More Americans Have College Degrees Than Ever Before. *The Hill.* Retrieved from https://thehill.com/homenews/state-watch/326995-census-more-americans-have-college-degrees-than-ever-before

Zientek, Linda. R., and Bruce Thompson. 2009. Matrix Summaries Improve Research Reports: Secondary Analyses Using Published Literature. *Educational Researcher, 38*(5). 343–352 doi: 10.3102/0013189X09339056

ACKNOWLEDGMENTS

To my husband, Ed: Thank you for being patient with me as I continue exploring my God-given purpose of educating others while I myself continue to learn.

To my daughters, Paige and Kendall: You both are boldly walking into the promises that the Word of God offers. I have been especially blessed to be called your mom.

I would also like to thank every individual who helped with this work by reading, editing, and offering insights. I am blessed to have you as part of my support network.

TESTIMONIALS

To say Dr. Stokes has been helpful would be an understatement. Dr. Stokes' ability to cut right to the heart of a matter and provide clear, concise, and relevant information has been extremely useful to me. At times I have felt overwhelmed. Dr. Stokes' encouraging and supportive voice, honed through her own practical experience, was exactly what I needed. Moving forward, I am now confident in knowing I can achieve my goals. Thank you, Dr. Stokes!

—Derek R.

In the final phase of the dissertation journey, there are so many small hurdles that have to be overcome. The guidelines and direction from Dr. Stokes have been a lifeline. Tips on reconciling references and on the various Microsoft features were particularly helpful. The directions were easy to follow. It saved me a lot of money by showing me how to edit my own dissertation.

—Linda W.

This guide is instrumental for anyone who desires to complete a doctoral journey successfully. The information contained within these pages will expand upon knowledge received from educational institutions and increase the success of learners. Dr. Stokes is a professional who cares about your success and your desire to complete this significant milestone. It is not difficult to tell that the words contained within this manuscript were written with love.

—Michelle T.

Your heavenly Father wants you to have a deep, meaningful relationship with Him. Consider the passage below and determine if you are ready to commit your everything to Him. He is waiting.

If you declare with your mouth, "Jesus is Lord," and believe in your heart that God raised him from the dead, you will be saved. For it is with your heart that you believe and are justified, and it is with your mouth that you profess your faith and are saved.

—Romans 10: 9–10 (NIV)

Printed in the United States
By Bookmasters